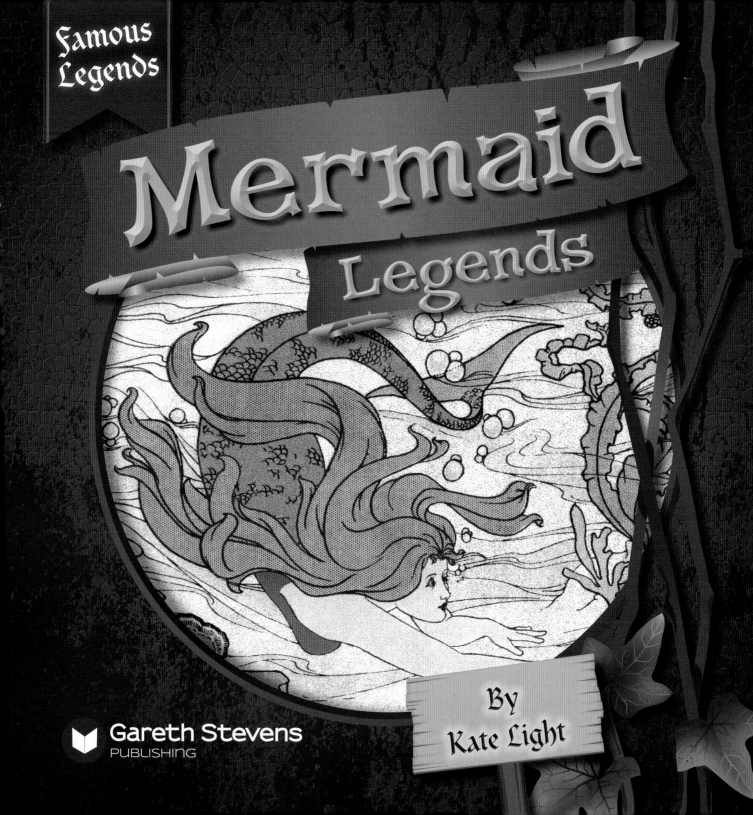

Famous Legends

Gareth Stevens PUBLISHING

Mermaid
Legends

By
Kate Light

Please visit our website, www.garethstevens.com. For a free color catalog of all our high-quality books, call toll free 1-800-542-2595 or fax 1-877-542-2596.

Cataloging-in-Publication Data

Names: Light, Kate.
Title: Mermaid legends / Kate Light.
Description: New York : Gareth Stevens Publishing, 2018. | Series: Famous legends | Includes index.
Identifiers: ISBN 9781538202449 (pbk.) | ISBN 9781538203811 (library bound) | ISBN 9781538203804 (6 pack)
Subjects: LCSH: Mermaids–Juvenile literature.
Classification: LCC GR910.L38 2018 | DDC 398.21–dc23

First Edition

Published in 2018 by
Gareth Stevens Publishing
111 East 14th Street, Suite 349
New York, NY 10003

Copyright © 2018 Gareth Stevens Publishing

Designer: Laura Bowen
Editor: Therese Shea

Photo credits: Cover, p. 1 (mermaid) whitemay/Getty Images; cover, p. 1 (forest) NEILRAS/Shutterstock.com; cover, p. 1 (ribbon) barbaliss/Shutterstock.com; cover, p. 1 (leather) Pink Pueblo/Shutterstock.com; cover, pp. 1–32 (sign) Sarawut Padungkwan/Shutterstock.com; cover, pp. 1–32 (vines) vitasunny/Shutterstock.com; cover, pp. 1–32 (parchment) TyBy/Shutterstock.com; cover, pp. 1–32 (background) HorenkO/Shutterstock.com; p. 5 DEA/DeAgostini/Getty Images; p. 7 (main) Csemerick/Wikimedia Commons; p. 7 (inset) Hazhk/Wikimedia Commons; p. 9 UniversalImagesGroup/Getty Images; p. 10 Electron/Wikimedia Commons; pp. 11, 13 ©iStockphoto.com/duncan1890; p. 14 Cerberoff/Shutterstock.com; p. 15 LaSylphide/Wikimedia Commons; p. 16 AFBorchert/Wikimedia Commons; p. 17 ©iStockphoto.com/Yuri_Arcurs; p. 19 Zew99/Wikimedia Commons; p. 21 (main) Philippe Lissac/GODONG; p. 21 (inset) Amcaja/Wikimedia Commons; p. 23 Magicgarden/Wikimedia Commons; p. 25 Blaine Image/Shutterstock.com; p. 27 (main) Felistoria/Wikimedia Commons; p. 27 (inset) M.violante/Wikimedia Commons; p. 29 (top) DEA/M. SEEMULLER/Getty Images; p. 29 (bottom) fzd.it/Shutterstock.com.

Printed in China

CPSIA compliance information: Batch #CS17GS: For further information contact Gareth Stevens, New York, New York at 1-800-542-2595.

Contents

Words in the glossary appear in **bold** type the first time they are used in the text.

Maidens and Monsters

What strange beasts could be hiding far below the ocean's waves? Many **cultures** pass down **legends** about monsters of the deep sea. Tales from all over the world tell of one special creature—the mysterious mermaid.

Mermaids are often said to be beautiful women who save drowning princes. But they're thought by some to be creepy monsters that **lure** humans into deadly traps. And in yet other legends, mermaids are something in between wicked and wonderful. Every mermaid legend is a tale you'll want to read!

The Inside Story

About 4,000 years ago, the Babylonians believed in a merman god named Ea. Atargatis was an ancient Syrian mermaid goddess honored more than 2,300 years ago.

This 19th-century work shows the Rhine daughters, who were female spirits of Germany's Rhine River. They're featured in some famous operas.

5

"The Little Mermaid"

One of the most famous mermaid stories in the world is Hans Christian Andersen's fairy tale "The Little Mermaid." You might know the Disney **version**, but Andersen's tale is very different. Here's a retelling:

Deep in the ocean, there lived a little mermaid who was curious about life on land. On her birthday, she swam to the surface for the first time and saw a handsome prince drowning. She carried him to shore, but hid before he woke up.

The Inside Story

Hans Christian Andersen was born into a poor family in Denmark in 1805. He made a name for himself with his tales, which included "The Emperor's New Clothes," "The Princess and the Pea," and "The Ugly Duckling."

This 1890 **illustration** by E. S. Hardy is a famous image of Hans Christian Andersen's little mermaid.

Hans Christian Andersen

The Painful Price of a Soul

Later, the little mermaid's grandmother told her that mermaids turn to bubbles in the sea after death, but humans have **immortal** souls. Her grandmother said she could receive a human soul if a human truly loved her. The little mermaid wanted to win the prince's love, but she needed legs to live in the human world. She asked a sea witch for help.

"I can give you legs," the witch said, "but you'll lose your tail and every step will feel like stepping on knives." Still, the little mermaid agreed.

The Inside Story

Andersen's sea witch had monsters called *polypi* outside her undersea house. They were half seaweed and half eel!

The sea witch gave the little mermaid a **potion** that made her tail split into legs.

Lost for Words

The sea witch required a terrible payment for the potion. She cut out the little mermaid's tongue and stole her voice! However, the potion worked. With her new legs, the mermaid joined the human world. Even though she couldn't speak, she and the prince became good friends.

One day, he told her, "I'm in love with the girl who saved my life. If only I knew who she was." Since the little mermaid couldn't speak, she couldn't tell the prince she was the girl!

The little mermaid and the prince spent all their time together.

A Deadly Deal

One day, the prince met a beautiful princess. He believed she was the girl who **rescued** him. The little mermaid was heartbroken. On the prince's wedding day, the mermaid's sisters swam close to the prince's ship.

"We traded our hair to the sea witch for this magical knife," they told her. "If you kill the prince, your tail will grow back and you can come home!" The mermaid took the knife, but she couldn't hurt her prince.

The Inside Story

The sea witch had told the little mermaid that she would die the morning after the prince married another. Still, the little mermaid couldn't kill the prince.

When the little mermaid saw the prince sleeping, she knew she couldn't kill him.

13

A Good Reward for a Good Deed

The little mermaid threw the knife into the sea, and the water turned red. She jumped into the water and burst into bubbles. Suddenly, she found herself in a bright, strange place. She was with the daughters of the air, who were a bit like angels.

The daughters said, "You're one of us because you **sacrificed** yourself for someone you love. Watch over human children with us, and you'll earn an immortal soul!"

At last, the mermaid was truly happy.

This is the last page of Hans Christian Andersen's first **draft** of "The Little Mermaid."

15

A Sea of Stories

European legends and fairy tales such as "The Little Mermaid" are very popular in books, movies, and art. In illustrations, mermaids usually look like kind and beautiful women with tails like fish.

However, mermaids in legends from other cultures have a range of appearances and powers. Each legend is **unique** to its culture, and you can learn a lot about a culture and its beliefs from its stories. Some legends can be quite scary!

About 71 percent of Earth is covered with water. It's no wonder there are so many legends of mysterious sea creatures!

Singing in the Trees

Rusalki are water spirits of Polish legend, and they can be deadly! They look like beautiful women, but live underwater. They're the ghosts of young women who were mistreated by men or who drowned. They climb willow trees and sing sweetly to lure men to their death.

According to legend, *rusalki* come onto land and dance in the moonlight at the beginning of summer. Any human who sees them is forced to join the dance—until they die!

The Inside Story

The opera *Rusalka* is somewhat like Hans Christian Andersen's "The Little Mermaid." However, in this story, the prince comes back and gives his life for the *rusalka* so she can have immortality.

Witold Pruszkowski's 1877 painting *Rusalki* hints at the deadly nature of these water spirits.

19

Mami Wata

One of the most famous African legends is Mami Wata, the powerful water spirit. Mami Wata means "Mother Water" or "Lady of the Water." Some people honor her as a goddess. She's often shown as a beautiful mermaid holding a snake.

Mami Wata can be kind or deadly, depending on the legend. In some stories, she lures people into the sea with her beautiful voice and drowns them. In others, she grants wishes, gives gifts, and heals the sick—but often at a price.

The Inside Story

Mami Wata is known as Mamba Muntu in central and east Africa. According to legend, if you steal her comb or a lock of her hair, she'll visit you in a dream. You can trade what you stole for a wish!

Mami Wata

Happyaku Bikuni

The mermaids of Japanese legends are called *ningyo*.

This is a retelling of a famous legend from the area of

Wasaka Bay in central Japan:

A fisherman once caught a *ningyo* and cooked it for

his friends. One saw the mermaid's face and told the others.

They were afraid to eat it, so they hid the meat in their

pockets. One of the friends had a daughter. She found the

meat in her father's

pocket later.

Thinking it was just

fish, she ate it.

The Inside Story

Ningyo means "human fish," but these creatures are often more like animals than humans. Some have fish bodies with ugly human faces, and others have monkey heads and fish tails.

This 18th-century illustration by Toriyama Sekien shows one version of a *ningyo*.

23

Peace at Last

No one knew right away, but the daughter stopped aging. The *ningyo* meat had given her a very long life. When her family and friends passed away, her long life became a lonely curse.

She decided to become a **Buddhist** priestess and traveled around, helping the poor and planting camellia flowers. After 800 years, she came home to Wasaka and passed away in a cave, finally at peace. When people told her story, they called her Happyaku Bikuni, or "800-year-old priestess."

The Inside Story

People visit Happyaku Bikuni's cave in Wasaka today, where camellia flowers still bloom. Some pray for health and long lives.

In legends, Happyaku Bikuni is sometimes called Yao Bikuni.

camellia
flowers

A Fishy Tale

In 1842, a man named Dr. J. Griffin claimed he discovered a mermaid. Circus owner P. T. Barnum placed it in his museum. People paid to see the "Feejee Mermaid," but what they really saw was a creepy—and fake—creature!

It turned out "Dr. Griffin" worked for P. T. Barnum. The two had set up one of the most famous mermaid **hoaxes** in history. The "Feejee Mermaid" had the head and upper body of a monkey sewed to the tail of a fish.

The Inside Story

In the 1500s, sailors made mermaid hoaxes using the dried bodies of sea animals called skates. These monster creations were called Jenny Hanivers.

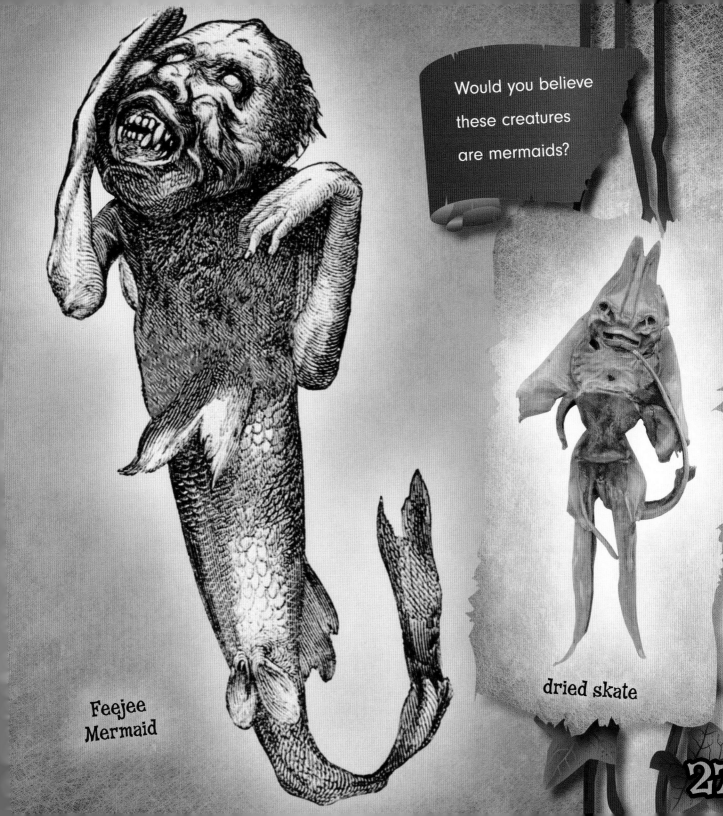

Would you believe these creatures are mermaids?

Feejee Mermaid

dried skate

27

The Legends Live On

Many people have reported seeing mermaids throughout history. Without the science we have today, it's understandable that a strange sea creature could be mistaken for a mermaid. In 2009, people reported seeing a mermaid off the coast of Israel. A town offered $1 million to anyone who took a photo of the mysterious creature, but no one did.

Are "sightings" like this honest mistakes or hoaxes, or could there be some truth to the stories told around the world? What do you believe?

The Inside Story

Christopher Columbus wrote about seeing ugly mermaids on his travels. Now we know they were actually just manatees!

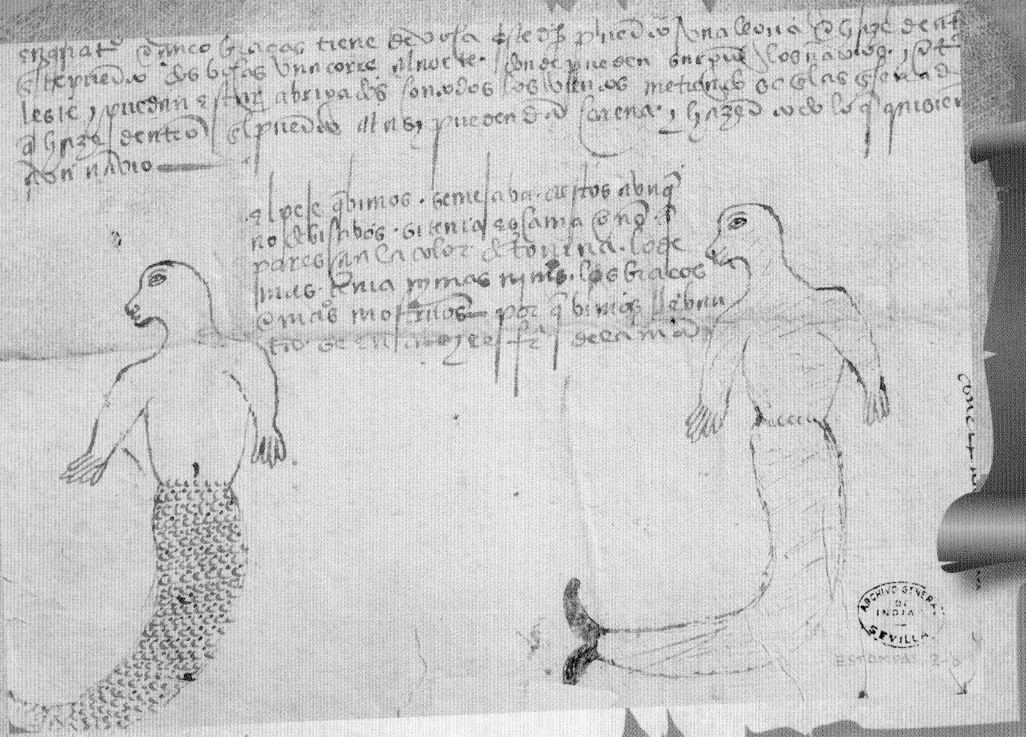

Spanish sailor Martin de Acosta drew these mermaids he said he saw in 1533.

manatees

Glossary

Buddhist: describing a system of beliefs from eastern and central Asia that is based on the teachings of Gautama Buddha

culture: a people with certain beliefs and ways of life

draft: a piece of writing that you make before the final version

hoax: an act meant to trick someone into believing something that is not true

illustration: a picture or drawing in a book

immortal: never dying

legend: a story from the past that is believed by many people, but cannot be proved to be true

lure: to draw an animal closer in order to catch it

potion: a drink that is meant to have a special or magical effect on someone

rescue: to save someone from danger

sacrifice: to give up something in order to get or do something else or to help someone

unique: very special or unusual

version: a story that is different in some way from another telling of the story

For More Information

Books

Forest, Heather. *Ancient & Epic Tales from Around the World.* Atlanta, GA: August House, 2016.

Hile, Lori. *Mermaids.* Chicago, IL: Capstone Raintree, 2013.

Loh-Hagan, Virginia. *Mermaids.* Ann Arbor, MI: Cherry Lake Publishing, 2017.

Websites

Are Mermaids Real?
oceanservice.noaa.gov/facts/mermaids.html
Check out what the National Oceanic and Atmospheric Administration says about this subject.

World of Tales
www.worldoftales.com
Explore more tales from around the world on this awesome site!

Index